My Science Library

Animal Adaptations

by Julie K. Lundgren

D1373110

Science Content Editor:
Kristi Lew

ROURKE CLASSROOM

www.rourkeclassroom.com

Science content editor: Kristi Lew
A former high school teacher with a background in biochemistry and more than 10 years of experience in cytogenetic laboratories, Kristi Lew specializes in taking complex scientific information and making it fun and interesting for scientists and non-scientists alike. She is the author of more than 20 science books for children and teachers.

www.rourkeclassroom.com

Project Assistance: The author also thanks Melissa Martyr-Wagner and Sam, Riley and Steve Lundgren.

Photo credits: Cover © Audrey Snider-Bell; Cover logo frog © Eric Pohl, test tube © Sergey Lazarev; Page 4 © hagit berkovich; Page 5 © Ammit; Page 6 © Eric Isselée; Page 7 © Geoffrey Kuchera; Page 9 © Jean-Edouard Rozey; Page 10 © Eric Isselée; Page 11 © Susan Flashman; Page 12/13 © Dirk Ercken; Page 15 © Audrey Snider-Bell; Page 16 © NREY; Page 17 © worldswildlifewonders; Page 19 © Sharon Day; Page 21 © Sari ONeal

Editor: Kelli Hicks

My Science Library series produced for Rourke by Blue Door Publishing, Florida

Library of Congress Cataloging-in-Publication Data

Lundgren, Julie K.
 Animal adaptations / Julie K. Lundgren.
    p. cm. -- (My science library)
 Includes bibliographical references and index.
 ISBN 978-1-61741-733-7 (Hard cover) (alk. paper)
 ISBN 978-1-61741-935-5 (Soft cover)
 1. Animals--Adaptation--Juvenile literature. I. Title.
 QL49.L956 2012
 591.5--dc22

                              2011003866

Rourke Publishing
Printed in China, Voion Industry
  Guangdong Province
042011
042011LP

www.rourkeclassroom.com - rourke@rourkepublishing.com
Post Office Box 643328 Vero Beach, Florida 32964

Table of Contents

Ways to Live

Adaptations help animals **survive**.

Some animals have colors that help them hide. Can you find the insect?

Big eyes help owls hunt at night.

5

Adaptations are ways animals have changed over many years. Adaptations include changes to animal bodies and actions.

Stinky spray drives away skunk enemies.

How Do I Look?

Some adaptations change how animals look. **Gills** allow fish to **breathe** underwater.

gill

9

Turtles have shells for protection.

Frogs' **webbed** feet help them swim.

How Do I Act?

Other adaptations change how animals act. Rattlesnakes shake their noisy tails to warn enemies.

tail

15

Lemurs use their tails for balance.

Chimpanzees use sticks to gather ants and **termites**.

A termite

19

One animal can have many adaptations to help it survive.

Horses have strong legs for running and long tails to shoo away flies.

21

SHOW What You Know

1. What kinds of adaptations do water animals have?

2. Do any land animals have the same adaptations as water animals?

3. Why are adaptations important?

Glossary

adaptations (ad-ap-TAY-shunz): changes in animals over time that help them live

breathe (BREETH): move fresh air in and used air out of the body

gills (GILLZ): the parts of a fish or other underwater animal used for breathing

survive (sur-VIVE): continue to live, in spite of dangers

termites (TUR-mites): small, soft insects that eat wood and live together in great numbers

webbed (WEBD): having skin that connects a finger or toe to its neighbor

Index

Websites

www.animalfactguide.com/

www.buildyourwildself.com/

www.ecokids.ca/pub/eco_info/topics/climate/adaptations/

About the Author

Julie K. Lundgren grew up near
Lake Superior where she liked to
muck about in the woods,
pick berries, and expand her rock
collection. Her interests
led her to a degree in biology.
She lives in Minnesota with
her family.